sticks and stones

and other poems

Marcia Muth

SANTA FE
NEW MEXICO

For Dr. Gail Kaplan
In appreciation for her friendship
and her interest in my work.

© 1993 by Marcia Muth

All Rights Reserved

No part of this book may be reproduced in any form or by any electronic or mechanical means including information storage and retrieval systems, without permission in writing from the publisher, except by a reviewer who may quote brief passages in a review.

First edition

Printed in the United States of America

Library of Congress Cataloging in Publication Data

Muth, Marcia, 1919-
    Sticks and stones and other poems / Marcia Muth. -- 1st ed.
      p. cm.
    ISBN 0-86534-214-8
    I. Title.
PS3563.U85S74   1993
811'.54--dc20   93-33309
                                                                   CIP

Published by Sunstone Press
                     Post Office Box 2321
                     Santa Fe, New Mexico 87504-2321 / USA

TABLE OF CONTENTS

Rock Crystal 5
Memo 5
Each Day 6
Morning Walk 7
The Fun House 8
Reflection 9
The Feather 9
The Satie Summer 10
First Snow 12
The Twisted Tree 12
Above 13
Moonwatch 13
I Have Seen 14
Now 15
Nearby An Owl Nests 16
This Morning 17
In Late October 17
Sticks and Stones 18
Observed 18
Run Off 19

Fall Days 20
Ravens 21
In the Sky 22
Those Little Gifts 22
May Evening 23
Runaway Rock 23
Mystic Circle 24
The Green Balloon 25
Summer's Garden 25
Tides 26
Sudden Shower 27
This Stone 28
After the Winter Carnival 29
The Ghost Dog 29
In the House 30
Restless Stones 30
The Apples of Winter 31
The Collector 31
One Last Time 32

ROCK CRYSTAL

Rock crystal
Rock music
Crystal set
Two halves
Of a life.

MEMO

Little scraps of paper
Lists
Memorials
To everyday life
Litter
Outlasting our thoughts

EACH DAY

When morning returns
Us to our natural state
We greet the world
Glad to be home,
Having been travelers
In the dark nighttime
Country of dreams
And strange adventures
For we are children
Of the sun and live
Only in its light.

MORNING WALK

I walk toward the mountains;
The morning wind, cool, brisk
Blows away the mist
From last night's dreams.
The dirt, stone-scattered road
Crunches under my feet;
Rabbits like stringed puppets
Jump away as I go past.
Blue jays signal my coming;
A raven's shadow touches me.

THE FUN HOUSE

In this house of mirrors
I see multiple reflections
Some thin, some fat
My image distorted
Now tall, now squeezed
Into smallness.
Head grotesque, huge
Long dangling arms;
I am returned
To early beginnings
Ape-person without a tree
To climb or vine to swing
Across broad sky.
I stare then run,
Somewhere there is an exit.

REFLECTION

Full-flavored and fleshy
The rounded peach
Cupped in my willing hand
Will not last, nor will I,
We are of this moment only
And then become memory.

THE FEATHER

The ancient Kachinas danced here
Early in the morning, very early
You can see their footprints
In the dust, soft and fading
Away as the sun comes
One day I found a feather
Where their shadows had been.

THE SATIE SUMMER

Do you remember that summer?
The cottage on the rocky cliff
Long wooden steps leading down
To the shore, sand, restless sea.
Who could forget those days,
Days of peace when David
Played Satie on the piano.

In the cottage, rooms were large
With darkened corners, ghost-catchers
Years of sand had scoured clean
Window sills and wooden floors.
Pictures were hung everywhere
A grandfather, stolid, stern
Unforgiving, perhaps unforgiven.
A soldier from the last war
Uncomfortable in his uniform
Does he hear our whispers of war
That drift in with the tide?
A picture of a ship slowly sinking
With sailors quickly drowning
Tactless, we think, looking
Out the windows to the sea.
We are uneasy at what we sense
But David at the piano and Satie
Charms all our fears away.

We have a treasure hunt
Through the cottage, finding relics
Of previous owners and visitors
Who have paused here for a time
Like shore birds who come and go.
Old magazines, a nature book
One roller-skate, a rolled-up flag
But no diaries, no letters
To give us facts, reliability
David finds an old black coat
Wrinkled, creased with age
He puts it on to play Satie.

In back there is an untidy garden
Its gradual ruin seems inevitable
We all make excuses for it.
In the evening, in candlelight
We sit with our backs to neglect
And face the understanding sea
While David plays Satie on the piano.

FIRST SNOW

The snow outlines
The tree limbs,
Graceful arrangement
In black and white.
Nature's own photo
Of winter season's
Fruitful coming.

THE TWISTED TREE

The twisted tree
Shaped by nature's hand
A reminder of transformation,
An act that comes
To us all in time;
That brittle cedar bark
My own aging hand.

ABOVE

The plane moves through the clouds
Its jet trail a wavy scribble
On the sky, childish drawing
The wind quickly erases.

MOONWATCH

We saw the moon, big and full
It filled our eyes with light.
Looking eagerly through the telescope
We were alone with the moon;
Earth on which we still stood
No longer existed as we stepped
Off into space and hovered over
The lunar landscape with its craters
Becoming as familiar to us now
As any of our best remembered landmarks.

I HAVE SEEN

I have seen
Grey whales swimming
In the Pacific deep;
Wind-robbed, rain-riddled
Caves of the cliff dwellers;
And the great rock shaped
Like a fish with one eye.
I have seen
The sun swallowed by the moon
Spit out again upon the sky;
How the restless stars
Wander from place to place
I have seen
All these many wonders
But not the heart of man.

NOW

Getting ready to close the
                door of summer
We begin to dream
            of hidden caves,
            the quiet places
Sun hours shorten; we look
To the moon for solace.
We are moved to near tears
By the subtle changes
In our landscape
            in our lives.

NEARBY AN OWL NESTS

You have to be silent and still
To see and hear the old mysteries
The small young fir tree clinging
To the side of the deepest canyon
Rocks older than man but more enduring
Little birds flying in big groups
Like schools of fish but skybound.
The sound of raven wings slapping
Softly against the clouded air
Wind that shifts the leaves
And gently lifts your eyelashes
This is a time for remembering
All those forgotten things
While nearby and owl nests.

THIS MORNING

The moon rests on the clouds
Indolent in the daytime sky
Perhaps still a little breathless
From the long night's march
Across our darkened world.

IN LATE OCTOBER

Once more the winter birds have come
Winging through cool, sterile air
Perching on bare-limbed trees
Eating our crusts and scattered seeds
But always keeping their own secrets.

STICKS AND STONES

Sticks and stones
Nature's own elements
Slender, fragile
Heavy, sturdy
Sticks break, bend
Weaving into patterns
Stones hard, strong
Building into shelters
Sticks and stones
The guardian spirits
Of our quiet places

OBSERVED

Today I saw you standing
In the park playground
Waiting there by the swings
Looking for a lost childhood
Or hoping for spring's return.

RUN OFF

In spring the mountain run off
Floods our nearby arroyo;
Strange things float down,
Some sticking in the mud
Clinging there like refugees
Tree limbs, bottles, cans
A chair, two legs missing
Bicycle wheel, bent and broken
Mismatched gloves, assorted shoes
A child's lost red jacket
Rocks and stones by the hundreds
Torn from their high home
To enhance our flat landscape.

FALL DAYS

Now that the leaves
Have fallen,
Harried to the ground
By autumn's winds
The birds perch in the
Stark, dry branches
Like dark, exotic blossoms
From some distant planet
Of the night

RAVENS

Who does not love ravens
Does not love life
Or understand the mysteries
Of our fast spinning planet;
Who does not hear
Whispers of eternity
In a raven's feathered
Flight across the land
Does not know beauty.

IN THE SKY

Hot air balloons
Cross our landscape
Rare flowers floating
On a celestial pond
And we, looking up,
Are amazed into silence
With a longing to escape
Our own earth ties.

THOSE LITTLE GIFTS

I go down to the beach afternoons
To see what the tide has brought
Those little gifts of the sea
Patterning the still damp sand.
Shells, delicate of design and color
Wood bits and pieces wave-shaped
Reminders of the passion and fury
Of a long-forgotten storm.

MAY EVENING

The moon lies like a thumb print
On the early evening sky
Faint but discernible,
Waiting quietly to begin
The long and lonely patrol
Across the darkened night.

RUNAWAY ROCK

This banded rock is history
Geology and part mystery
Small enough to hold in one hand
Yet matching in color and shape
The close surrounding cliffs.
A runaway rock, centuries old
Would not be happy on my shelf
Or content to live indoors;
I put it back along the path,
A little monument to the past.

MYSTIC CIRCLE

Stonehenge
The past displayed
Though not revealed.
What giant hands
At play there
On Salisbury Plain
Balanced these forms,
Planned the mystic circle
And then left,
Called away
Or bored by blocks
Went home to lunch
Or nap.

THE GREEN BALLOON

The small balloon floats overhead
A stranger in our sky, a fugitive
Lifted from a child's fragile hand
By a sudden unkind burst of wind
Now free, round, glossy and green
It follows some secret map lines
Known usually only to the birds
And like them comes to rest at last
At the top of the tallest of trees.

SUMMER'S GARDEN

Now that winter snow has melted
I look with renewed vision
At my small, intimate landscape
Whose boundary trees hint gently
Of the coming of warmth, spring.
In my mind, I plan summer's garden
Colorful, flourishing, ripening
Into rich goodness and joy.

TIDES

There are tides
That stir stones
To movement
Times when they
May move and turn
When mountains rise
And boulders fall
Obedient to some
Universal law.

SUDDEN SHOWER

The rain comes up suddenly
Not heavy but lightly
So I walk between the drops
That bounce on the ground
And spatter on the border stones
With random dot patterns.
Moving under the dark cloud
I climb to the top of a hill
And see the next valley
Resting, cupped in sunshine.

THIS STONE

This stone
I hold in my hand
A symbol
Of the ages,
Revolving
From earth-cold
To palm-warm
Reminds me
I am a newcomer,
New-born form
In an eternal
Sea of time.

AFTER THE WINTER CARNIVAL

The ice sculptures are melting
Under the warming January sun;
King Neptune returns to water,
The sharp, carved castle turrets
Where Beauty and the Beast reigned
Now are rounded and slope
Toward the waiting ground;
And the lion made with such care
Slowly shrinks to a kitten.
Winter carnival has ended
For them and for us also
As we turn our hearts to spring.

THE GHOST DOG

The Ghost Dog waits along the trail;
Runs sniffing at the heels of travelers.
He came with the first explorers,
Winter froze them out; they left
But still filled with hope, he waits
Guarding the last summer's camp.

IN THE HOUSE

A single leaf
Blown in by the wind
Or carried in
By a careless shoe.
One leaf only,
Red and sere;
Autumn's hand print
On our carpet.

RESTLESS STONES

Some rocks and stones travel
Jumping over fences and gates
Leaving familiar green gardens
Crossing over ponds and rivers
Sliding down steep mountains.
I find them on my walks,
Pausing on their long journey
To taste our dirt and rain.

THE APPLES OF WINTER

The apples that unheeded
           dropped and dried
Under the winter sun
Are now swept up in spring's
           careful raking
Shrunken, patterned, whorled
They are like fossils
Of strange sea creatures
Yet curiously light
           to my touch.

THE COLLECTOR

I collect rocks and stones
The way some others save
Stamps, coins or shells.
Small hand-holding stones
Warming in my palm;
Smooth river-washed rocks
Sleek as the backs of seals
And rough-edged ones
Like small locked fortresses
Unknown universes, foreign
Holding their own secrets.

ONE LAST TIME

The last day at the beach
We build larger sand castles
           Collect more shells
And take longer walks
Letting the seaweed drift
           Around our feet
We stand and sniff the air
           Wanting to remember
The hot sun, the salt smell
           The surf sounds
As waves roll up against us.
Then in evening, after dark
We will dress up and go
           Along the boardwalk
Down to the lights and music
           Of the Dance Pavilion
And later watch the rising moon
Reflect itself in the restless
           Dark night sea.

www.ingramcontent.com/pod-product-compliance
Lightning Source LLC
Chambersburg PA
CBHW051706040426
42446CB00009B/1327